How To Hunt For High Quality Freebie Products and Services Online

I0482189

HTeBooks

Copyright © 2016

Disclaimer

This book is designed to provide condensed information. It is not intended to reprint all the information that is otherwise available, but instead to complement, amplify and supplement other texts. You are urged to read all the available material, learn as much as possible and tailor the information to your individual needs.

Every effort has been made to make this book as complete and as accurate as possible. However, there may be mistakes, both typographical and in content. Therefore, this text should be used only as a general guide and not as the ultimate source of information. The purpose of this book is to educate.

The author or the publisher shall have neither liability nor responsibility to any person or entity regarding any loss or damage caused, or alleged to have been caused, directly or indirectly, by the information contained in this book.

Table of Contents

HOW WILL THIS BOOK HELP YOU? 4

EVERYTHING YOU NEED TO KNOW ABOUT FREEBIE PRODUCTS AND SERVICES ONLINE 5

HOW TO GET FREE STUFF FROM AMAZON 14

GET COMPANIES TO SEND YOU FREEBIES 18

HOW TO SCORE HIGH QUALITY FREEBIES ONLINE 26

HOW TO APPLY WHAT YOU'VE LEARNED? 32

How Will This Book Help You?

There are a million and one ways to get free things. At the top of my mind, one of these ways is getting gifts from loved ones. But have you ever wondered whether there could actually be another way you could get free stuff? If you have, you're in luck because in this book, we shall focus on how to get high quality freebie products and services online.

This book will equip you with everything you need to go from a freebie-hunting novice to a freebie-hunting master who knows how to get the best high-end devices and services.

This book will give you free resources you can instantly use to snatch online freebies in an instance. It will also outline the steps you need to take to get freebies from your favorite companies.

If you're excited to get started, let's get right to it.

Everything You Need To Know About Freebie Products and Services Online

"The truly free man is the one who can turn down an invitation to dinner without giving an excuse."

- Jules Renard

The term "free" usually means different things to all of us. To some, it means getting something without paying for it. To others, it may mean getting a free sample gift at the local supermarket. Unfortunately, most of us are enormously cynical of the products we refer to as "free", and always look out for their hidden costs. For example, when you go to the local mart and a company-hired marketer offers to give you a gift, you're always quick to ask, "what's the catch?"

It's not hard to find out the origin of this cynicism. In business, free is not used in the same context as most of us interpret it. In fact, marketers use the 'science of freebies' to lure customers in. What type of freebies do you desire? Do you want freebies that have caveats to them? Or do you want freebies that have zero strings attached to them? My guess is that you fall in the latter category.

Now, I must say and point out that while there are many mega companies bustling to give you freebies, it is highly unlikely that you'll get to enjoy these gifts until you understand how freebies and freebies sites work. Let us do that now.

As indicated, most companies giving out freebies do so in the form of promotions and giveaways to consumers like you. Although the gifts present themselves as loyalty gifts, i.e. gifts you receive for "being loyal to the brand", the company giving this freebie expects to retain you as their client so that you can test other 'new' or 'old' products they may have and also so that you may market their products when and if you like them. In this case, the companies do not expect you to join their marketing team, no. They simply expect that since you like their product, and they have used a freebie of some sort to show you that you're a valued consumer, you will use word of mouth to recommend their products to your immediate circle.

These companies use the marketer's reciprocity principle. They use your sense of obligation to a good brand and the gifts they give you to motivate you to buy more and market them more.

Although this principle works extremely well for brick and motor companies with physical products, it also works extremely well for online products and services. However, for the online market, the idea has been tweaked and turned into freebie websites. What are freebies websites?

A freebie site is any directory or platform that lists free products that various companies have put up for grabs.

What you should note is that a freebie site does not give you free stuff; they merely give you information on what free product samples companies are offering. Freebie sites inform you as the visitor, what you need to do to claim the company's offer.

If you've been keen, you should have noted that when you click on a free sample link on most sites, that link redirects you to another site where you sign up for the freebie. This means, freebie sites are the third parties. They just direct you and leave the deal between you and advertising website. Think of them as messengers who find for you the companies giving out freebies and inform you about their freebies.

As you may have already guessed, there are many companies ready to offer you freebies. In fact, today, you can get high-end freebies such as gadgets, books, movies etc.

However, before you run out to start your freebie hunting adventure, you should know that even though thousands of companies offer gifts online and offline, the 'freebie industry' is not a free for all market. In fact, out of the thousands of people prospecting for high-end quality freebies, only a small percentage of them get the actual gifts.

I'm sure you're wondering, "what's so special about the small percentage that gets these freebies, or what it is that they do different so as to receive these gifts?"

The answer is simple: those who get freebies online are privy to some of the best principles and strategies you should follow and use to get freebies. Before we outline the strategies you can use to snag your high quality freebies, let us look at some guiding principles every 'freebie hunter' should follow.

The Three Freebie-Hunting Commandments

#1- Thou shall be pragmatic- Although the best things in life are free, don't quit your day job to become a full time online freebie prospector. Although you can get tons of free things online, it is very unlikely that the freebies will make you rich.

#2- Thou shall not sell your freebies online-When you succeed in getting free stuff, which you will, don't sell it for profit. Putting your freebies on craigslist or e-bay is equal to opening a can of legal worms.

#3- Thou shall be honest- When you receive a free product that you don't like, be decent enough not to recommend it to others.

Now that you have rules to follow as you prospect for online freebies, let us examine strategies that should guide your freebie-prospecting mission.

Freebie Scoring Strategies

There are many ways of scoring online freebies. Unfortunately, getting high quality freebies is not always easy. For example, CNET gets many high-end tech freebies; CNET is a technology review website. In fact, whenever a new technological device hits the market, they are usually the first ones to test it and write a comprehensive review about that product.

However, for them to get to where they are, they have had to do certain things. For example, CNET is a review website. Which means, for them to get to where they are, they have had to buy devices (they get them for free now, but they didn't always use to), test them and write a review that helps other people who may be interested in that particular device. That is CNET's strategy for scoring freebies. Let me ask you something; what is your freebie scoring strategy? Do you even have one?

The truth is that, until you formulate a strategy, there will be no difference between you and the thousands of people who have tried to score high-end freebies year in year out to no avail. You must create your strategy.

Your strategy will guide you to the freebies of your choice. Unless you're willing to put in the time and snag freebies the hard way, i.e. substitute your time for a high-end freebie (this is the same thing CNET did; they spend their time reviewing devices and writing reviews and in return, they get free high end tech devices). You need to create a strategy that guides you to where the freebies are instead of chasing the freebies all year round.

Your freebie strategy will depend on what types of freebies you desire and what you're willing to do to get them. To create your freebie strategy, follow the prompts below.

Keep your eyes and ears open.

You need to be well informed of all available freebie opportunities. Freebies won't just fall into your lap. In fact, if you know about Tom Locke and his $39 experiment(http://www.the39dollarexperiment.com/), you know that out of the many companies that offer freebies, only a few of them will offer you freebies. Don't' just sit around and wait for companies to send you emails or letters of the freebies they are offering. Stalk (in a good way) all your favorite companies on social media and in the news to know when these companies offer freebies to their loyal customers. Keep your eyes and ears open to any places that may be offering the freebies of your choice. For example, many radio stations often give out quality freebies for commenting, liking, and sharing their status updates on social media. At the same time, when Microsoft, Samsung or Apple announces new devices; there are tons of companies offering these devices for free.

Choose wisely

Before you sign the dotted line and opt in to a freebie, pay attention to the fine print. Look to see whether there are limitations or catches. Sometimes some offers are indeed too good to be true. Some companies may indicate that they're giving out a free TV or car but at the end of it they ask for your credit card and then charge you an exuberant shipping fee that to compensate them for the TV or car.

When most companies do their marketing, they tend to ask for your demographic information such as, medical condition, income, or size of household. Be cautious not to give out any personal information to them.

Create a secondary email address

Sometimes, companies give out birthday freebies or coupons to consumers who like them on social media or who are signed up for that company's mailing list. Fortunately, you can join as many company mailing lists as you want. However, to separate your emails; it's good practice to create a separate email account before signing up for any freebie online. This ensures that you only disclose the information you're comfortable with. It will also ensure that your freebie email alerts and important personal emails stay separate. Create one email account dedicated to any online freebie opt-in.

Act quickly

Many high quality freebies tend to be available on limited supply. Moreover, their availability is highly dependent on how fast the word spreads. Today, with the increased use of social media, word of high quality freebies spreads very fast. When you see high-end freebies, waste no time. Snatch them fast before someone else does.

Remember to have some fun

I assume you're not a professional freebie enthusiast. If you're not, remember not to get angry when you ask Channel to send you a free sample of their signature cologne and they flatly tell you to buy your own. It is highly unlikely that all the companies you email or ask to send you free samples will. Remember to have fun with this. When a company says "no", simply move on to the next one. There are thousands of companies just waiting for you to ask them for freebies.

*Key point/action step

The first step to getting any online freebie is a strategy. A strategy determines how you hunt for freebies. For example, you cannot hunt for a freebie you can't see. To snag high quality freebies, you need information. Where and how you get this information forms the crux of why you need a strategy. Fortunately, you now have everything you need to create a strategy.

How To Get Free Stuff From Amazon

"… You basically have a license to drive a Hummer through the Amazon"

- Thomas Friedman

Yes! Amazon is a free for all freebie market. If you're a frequent Amazon shopper, you've probably seen the thousands of users writing awesome positive reviews on products. Although most of these people are customers who've bought an item and left an informative review to help others, a big percentage of these people, i.e. the many people writing Amazon reviews do so in return for a free product.

In fact, at this particular moment, there are probably thousands of companies with Amazon store just baying for people to write them reviews in exchange for free sample gifts. This could be you today! You may be wondering why Amazon would want to give out free stuff. After all, they're in the business of making money, right? Well, the answer is simple: Amazon FBA (https://services.amazon.com/fulfillment-by-amazon/benefits.htm).

Amazon has made it tremendously easy for anyone to sell products warehoused and shipped through their FBA program. Now, if we were to go back to our marketing knowledge, we know that in the online space, products with more reviews tend to outdo products with lesser reviews.

This is extremely good news for you because, on a daily basis, Amazon receives hundreds of new products to include in their fulfillment program. Most of these products can be yours through two ways:

Hard way

There are two ways to get things freely from Amazon; first is by being part of them. Amazon invites "vine voice" community members to contribute to reviews in exchange for gifts. If we're being honest, this way is not that ideal because you have to trade in your time and write a bunch of helpful reviews before they can even think about inviting you to their program.

That is the first way of getting Amazon to give you free stuff. The second way is the easy way...

Easy Way

Amazon has many digital nomads listing their products on the store. Most if not all of these companies use a service referred to as Tomoson(https://www.tomoson.com/about-tomoson/features) to find people i.e. normal people like you and me to whom they can send their free products to in exchange for some word of mouth hype.

Most of these companies often tend to give out a 100% off coupon code for their items, or ask you to buy their products and they reimburse you for it. Either way, all you need to do is to leave a review of these products and voila! That item is yours to keep, forever!

To get started, sign up for their account to get access to their products. After creating your account, link it with your social media account. After this, head over to blogger or WordPress and create a free blog to start writing reviews and sharing them on social media.

Coincidentally, every day, a ton of new Amazon review sites pop up everywhere. While you may have zero experience with them and the freebies they offer, they follow the Amazon concept. You should realize that every day, dozens of online sellers are willing to offer you their product freely if you're willing to write a review. In fact, some of them don't require a twitter or blog; just the Amazon review. Take advantage of this.

You probably may be wondering, "Why should I bother with Amazon?" Here is why. Although you have to trade in your time for a free product (writing the review), due to the sheer number of high end freebies available and the multi-national companies willing to give you their products in exchange for a review, Amazon is worth the effort. In fact, if you build a good website that has helpful reviews, Tomoson will not hesitate to give you the latest iPhone or Samsung Galaxy if they think it will give the phone some much needed social sharing.

*Key point/action step

Although it may not seem like it, thousands of people receive freebies from Amazon every day. All you have to do is sign up, choose your gift, receive it and write a comprehensive review geared to help people. Of course, the company wants a positive review.

However, if there's something specific you hate about a product, make sure to point out in the product cons.

Get Companies To Send You Freebies

"We must free ourselves of the hope that the sea will ever rest. We must learn to sail in high winds."

- Aristotle Onassis

To get a company to send you free products, you must do something in return. They say that 'fortune favors the brave'. Although this may sound very far from our topic of discussion, to get companies to send you free stuff, you have to take broad steps such as joining rewards program, taking surveys, complaining about a product, or requesting free samples. In fact, getting companies to send you free stuff is that simple. All it requires is the following steps.

Method 1: Complain about a product

As a consumer, you have a right to complain about any product or service that has not met your demand. This is natural and something meant to guarantee equal treatment and services. You can also complain your way to free products. However, it is only best to complain about items, products, and services that fall short of their advertising glory. Complaining your way to free products does not mean becoming like the very famous British woman who rakes in 200 USD of products in a month by bombarding companies with complain mail concerning poor services and products. There is a right and a wrong way to complain to companies. Here is how to go about it

Step 1: Complain about a product you want

You cannot just pop out a deceitful complain and expect to receive a freebie just like that. You should have a reasonable complain that is worth compensation. For example;

If you're in a hotel where you're served a cup of coffee but notice a dead fly floating inside your mug of coffee, that is a complain worth compensating. The same principle applies to the online space. If an online service or product is below the standards you would expect in a related product, you have a right to complain and get reimbursed with a new free product.

Step 2: Locate the company's contact info

How are you going to reach out to the company you want to complain to? Are you going to reach out via email postal address, etc.? Fortunately, you can easily locate most company email addresses on their product packages. If this seems tedious, you can always go to that company's website.

Step 3: Communicate with the company

After getting the company's number or email address, contact them and let them know about your displeasure with a specific product. Include your proof of purchase in your complaint. Be persistent without being rude and ask them to replace the products by giving you a gift card

Step 4: Be patient

Keep calm and wait for your freebies. Most companies will placate you with a flattering replacement item or a redeemable voucher for a free item. Most companies will also reply to your mail to thank you for the continued support and input.

Method 2: Join rewards schemes

This is another simple way of wining yourself freebies. Most big companies have a reward team that rewards consumers for their royalty. Freebies on a reward scheme can sometimes be invaluable. Don't mind this. Make a point of finding out if your favorite company has a reward scheme you can join. Here is a systematic guide on how to rake it big with rewards schemes.

Step 1: Find rewards program

Members of a rewards team have access to product vouchers, coupons, discounts off on purchasing or points towards different prizes. After you find out if your company has a rewards team, join and enjoy the advantages.

Step 2: Join numerous programs

The more reward teams you join the more free items and discounts you'll get. For instance, if you join various grocery stores reward teams, one of them might be rewarding their consumers with free items today and another one tomorrow. This may place you at an advantage.

Step 3: Focus on one credit card rewards scheme

If a reward scheme is offering free credit cards to win points and redeem them for items, concentrate on a single card to increase your points. Doing this will maximize your points and thus maximize your point to free gift ratio.

Step 4: Redeem rewards before expiry

Most rewards have a limited life expectancy. You may intend to target the accumulation of points to a certain level before redeeming for a favored item only to discover that your points expired long before you could use them. Unless you are sure your rewards have no expiry date, always redeem them as soon as possible.

Method 3: Take surveys

Most people tend to think that taking surveys for freebies is not a cool or legit way of getting online freebies. Part of the reason for this is because there are many scam survey sites coning people of their hard earned cash. To ensure you don't fall prey to this bogus sites, follow the following steps.

Step 1: Keep your receipts

Most stores nowadays have a websites where consumers can complete surveys about shopping or dining experience. Their gifts in most cases are gift card or vouchers, a cash prize or a discount on your next shopping after completing the survey. If you visit most company websites, a pop up window may pop up prompting you to take a survey about your user experiences with that company. Don't hesitate to take the survey if the window promises to compensate your time with free stuffs or coupons.

Step 2: Get paid to take surveys

Most companies offer consumer surveys. The companies tend to do this to get product feedback and to advertise their products. You can find some of these companies online. In fact, there are thousands of legit online companies and websites offering cash for surveys. Ipsos survey panel(http://www.i-say.com/) is a very good example. Sign up and start taking their surveys. If they pick you to complete more in-depth surveys, you might end up receiving free items from various companies.

Method 4: Request free samples

You can get free samples from various companies depending on how you explain your need for the sample or how you choose to approach the company. Most well established companies give out their products samples to their consumers for product testing or for marketing purposes.

To win yourself free sample items, try this out;

Step 1: Write a letter to the company

When writing a letter to a company in the hope of snagging free samples, focus on telling them how their company and products rock. You can also try to tilt the odds of winning freebies by adding a personal experience story to the brand. For example, if you want a free product from a toy manufacturer, let them know you have used their products before and you loved their products. This will show the company that you know about their other products and have used them. The trick to pulling this off is being enthusiastic and specific as much as you can.

Request for free products by asking the company whether they have any free coupons or samples for their loyal consumers.

Step 2: Start a product review blog

If you write product's review for specific companies on your blog, asking that company to send you their free samples for review purposes is very easy. Most companies will give you free products for free publicity on your blog.

*Key point/action step

Truthfully, getting companies to send you products is not always easy. However, if you're persistent, take rejection with a pinch of sugar and a lot of goofiness, you will undoubtedly rake in those high quality freebies you've been searching for. The trick to getting companies to send you free stuff is by connecting with them on a personal level.

How To Score High Quality Freebies Online

"I know where I'm going and I know the truth, and I don't have to be what you want me to be. I'm free to be what I want"

- Muhammad Ali

They say chance favors the bold. By being bold, you can easily get free gadgets, entertainment, free travel, and even free internet access by knowing a few easy tips and tricks. Here are a few of these tips and tricks guaranteed to get you access to high quality freebies.

Gadgets

Almost all consumer gadgets are often in high demand. This makes it a bit difficult but not impossible to get high quality gadgets.

To receive free consumer electronic, you require a little bit of ingenuity. Nevertheless, it is important to keep your expectations in check. Getting free gadgets will require you to sacrifice some of your choices. For example, you may be focusing on an iPad as a freebie. While this is ok, it is not a feasible focus because often times, stores, or companies rarely ever give out the latest product. In fact, as you prospect for high-end free devices, you should note that often times, you would have to compromise and go for a lesser product model.

There are various ways to go about snagging high quality freebies. Here are a few of these ways

Write reviews

For years now, I've been exchanging reviews for high-end devices such as PlayStation, cell phones, etc. For me, it started with one Amazon review where after Amazon noted that my reviews helped many people on the site, they invited me to join a private program referred to as Vine.

Through this program, Amazon sends out a newsletter accompanied by new products offered by different companies to me every few weeks. Every member of Vine can claim any product for free as long as it is still available. In return, Vine members are required to write a review. This is something you can do today to get free books, gadgets and more. All you have to do is write helpful reviews. Fortunately, we've already looked at how to become a member of vine and get free things almost anytime you want to.

Appreciate and acquire the gadgets of the past

Everyone wants the latest gadgets. This makes them a bit difficult to come by in the freebie world. If you accept older tech items, such as old iPhones, you can always find them on sites such as, Craigslist and Freecycle(http://www.freecycle.com/). Everything on Freecycle is free. On craigslist, you will have to search for $0 items or search for terms such as "free" and "curb alert." You can also go to craigslist main page and click on the 'free' section. In addition, craigslist provides a web tool that alerts you whenever they have free gadgets.

How to acquire free movies, books and other media

If finding free gadgets appears to be tricky, finding free movies, books and other media happens to be simpler. It requires less of your work and gives you a fair number of choices. Below are your options:

Keep writing reviews

When you become a helpful online reviewer and gain access to Amazon Vine, you have at your disposal different ways to acquire free music, movies, and books. If you're looking for the best books, I suggest you try Google Good reads.

Find free books online

There are many free books online offered by "Google Books" in form of text and audio. There is an app called Kindle; if you install it in your device, you can get public domain books free from Amazon. All you need is to search and download whatever you want.

How To Stop Paying For Phone And Internet Services

Phone services and internet access should not cost you anything since you can get both free. All it takes you is signing up for the right services. Here are a few tips.

Acquire free broadband internet services with FreedomPop(https://www.freedompop.com/)

Accessing broadband internet tends to be expensive. However, with Freedom pop, it will cost you a deposit of $100, which you can get back after you cancel your service.

When you sign up for the service on your phone, it will turn your mobile into a Wifi hotspot that will provide reasonably data connection that is fast even when serving five computers through WiMAX network. By default, they offer you 500mb on a monthly basis. In case you complete your offer, you can earn extra data that is fantastic for casual browsing or on occasional on-the-go connection.

Make calls free to US and Canada using Gmail

As long as you can access the internet, you don't have to pay for your phone calls. Gmail offers free calling via Google voice to Cell phones and landlines between Canada and the United States. All you have to do is to create a Gmail account and have an active internet connection and you can talk as much as you want for free.

Travel free

Travelling is not cheap. However, by taking advantage of frequent flier programs and using a few tricks, you can knock down those entire travel costs. To travel free, you have to do bit of work, but almost everybody can earn discounts with minimal effort. Here are a few hacks to help you out:

Sign up for travel programs and reward cards at the right time

We all know that to earn frequent flier miles using credit cards that offer bonuses requires thousands of dollars and thousands of in-flight hours to earn a round trip flight. Delta or Star Alliance Airlines, have branded travel credit cards that offers you 25000-30000 points when you sign up and make one purchase. That's equals to free ticket.

To kick your mileage balance airline credit cards are the best. American airline offers 75000 miles after you purchase their branded credit card, Virgin Atlantic offers 50,000 and United offers 40000. Get one of these travel credit cards and gain free miles the best and quickest way.

*Key point/action step

It is crucial to remember that free isn't really free. You might not be paying with your money, but you are paying with information, effort or something else. In some cases, the sacrifices you make are worthwhile, but generally know what exactly you are sacrificing.

How to Apply What You've Learned?

At this particular moment, you have everything you need to start high end, quality freebies and services. However, remember that the type of freebies you get depends on your strategy. For example, to get the latest tech devices, your best bet is by going with reviewing your way to them. Remember: your freebie hunting strategy is very important. Create one adhering to the principles and commandments we listed in chapter one.

Amazon is a free for all freebie for those who know how to run through the freebie maze. Getting free stuff from Amazon requires reviews. The best thing about Amazon is their invitation only Vine program. The trick to being great at Amazon reviews is creating witty and honest reviews.

Every day, thousands of companies send freebies to their consumers. Getting companies to send you the item is not always easy, but with a clear contact strategy (preferably an enthusiastic message that paints you as the most enthusiastic consumer that company has), snagging freebies from companies is easy.

Unfortunately, free is not always free. When opting in to a free offer, make a point of reading the fine print. Know exactly what you're getting into before you get into it. After all, a bit of cynicism never hurt anyone.

www.ingramcontent.com/pod-product-compliance
Lightning Source LLC
Chambersburg PA
CBHW070427190526
45169CB00003B/1447